MellonCollie Ravings of a Dyslexic Poet

William Fraser (Pesky Poetry)

PeskyPoetry™
2022

Copyright © 2022 by Pesky Poetry Publishing

All rights reserved. This book or any portion thereof may not be reproduced or used in any manner without the express written permission of the publisher except for use of brief quotations in a referencing format.

PeskyPoetry, PeskyPoet and all variants thereof are the Copyright of William Fraser and subject to a Trademark.

Cover artwork by Matthew J Hill of The Caterpillar Shivered© commissioned by Pesky Poetry for this book. Artwork is subject to copyright.

First Print: 2020

Reprint: 2022

ISBN 978-1-7396901-0-6

PeskyPoetry (info@peskypoetry.co.uk)

www.peskypoetry.com

Dedication

I would like to dedicate this book to my late grandfather. A man of many talents and the father figure who made me the person I am today.

The world is darker,
The air is colder,
Now that you are not here.
I will go on,
With all that you taught me,
Without fear.
You will be missed,
Each and every day,
Until we meet again.

Poems

Dedication 15
Acknowledgements 12
Forward 13
    Dyslexia Is A Blessing Not A Curse 13
The MelonCollie 14
Pets 15
    The Potato Hider 15
    Black Spot 16
    A Smudge on Our Hearts 17
    Our Little Star 18
    Living to the Max 19
    Soft Sophie 20
    The Sock Stealer 21
    Our Little Poppy 22
    Storm in a Teacup 23
    Garfield 24
    Love so Skye High 25
Animals 26
    Cat Among The Pigeons 26
    Ladybug 27
    Lion 28
    Seagull 29
    Humans 30
    Platypus 31
    Cat 32
    Mouse 33

Dog	34
Magpie	35
Caterpillar	36
Dragonfly	37
Flowers	38
Daffodil	38
Rose	39
Dandy Lion	40
Lily	41
Daisy	42
Tulip	43
Thistle	44
Rhododendron	45
Fruit Rhyme	46
What is a Fruit	46
Strawberry	47
Pomegranate	48
Banana	49
Banana (ALT)	50
Kiwi	51
Tomato	52
Cherry	53
Lime	54
Durian	55
Lemon	56
Pineapple	57
Pineapple (ALT)	58
Lemons and Life	59

Temporary Things 60
  Sea Wave 60
  Bubble 61
  Life 62
  Winer Frost 63
  Summer Breeze 64
  Seasons 65
  Fireworks 66
  Time 67
  Underneath These Stars 68
  The Simple Things 70
  Ode to the Elements 71
  Earth ▽ 71
  Air △ 72
  Fire △ 73
  Water ▽ 74
  Metal 75
  Wood 76
Love Poems 77
  Another Time or Another Place 77
  You're one of a Kind 78
  Why I Love the UK 79
  Acrostic Love Poem 80
  I Dream 81
  I Am a Lucky Man 82
  Hope 83
  What I Would Give 84

This Old Heart of Mine 85
Open That Tin Heart 87
Light of My Life 88
Today I Thought Of You 89
If Life Were 90
Te Amo 91
Winter of Love 92
Love Is Like a Song 93
We Once Said I Love You 94
Will Boys Just Be Boys 95
For You 96
All I Want 97
Love Is 98
Love Is Like 99
Sometimes All You Need Is Hello 100
I Learned To Love From You 101
Love for the Now 102
Guide Me Through 103
You Make the World Simple 104
Acrostic Valentine Request 105
Better To Have Loved and Lost 106
You Are Wonderful 107
Give Me a Movie 108
Crime of Love 109
Mines Is a Redhead 110
My Love for You 111
Keep an Open Heart 112
Love (Read between the Lines) 113

Letting Go Of Love 114
Affirmation of Love 115
You Were My Dream 116
Weak at the Knees 117
He FriendZoned Me 118
The Last Words (Before the First Kiss) 119
Oddity of Love 120
Love in Actions 121
I Will Always Love You 122
Just Wish I Could Ask 123
Words of Love 124

Letters 125
   To A Loving Mum 125
   To My Special Man 126
   To An Old Crush 127
   To My Late Dad 128
   Goodbye to another Family Member 129
   To A Loving Family 130
   To My Dog 131
   To The One My Heart Wants 132
   To The One That Got Away 133

The End 134
   Last But Not Least 134

About The Author 135

Acknowledgements

There are three main acknowledgements I would like to make.

Firstly, to my partner, without whom, the name and the excitement behind this book would not have happened.

Secondly, to Matthew Hill of The Caterpillar Shivered, whose penmanship brought the MelonCollie to life.

Thirdly, to my readers, for keeping me going with your lovely comments and reading of my works. Without you, this would be pointless.

My love for you will never fade,
And grows deeper day-by-day,
Never change who you are,
My brightly shining shooting star.

Forward

So someone should probably explain the title... *MelonCollie Ravings of a Dyslexic Poet*.

The name has an origin,
Like so many do,
And here I shall,
Share it with you.
A dyslexic mind,
Has magic inside,
Creating things,
Others won't find.
Fireplaces become Firepalaces,
The act of tiring becomes tyreing,
And being melancholy becomes a MelonCollie.
While reviewing old poems,
These mistakes came to light,
And reminded me why I wright.
Dyslexia isn't a curse,
Or something to hide,
It's a blessing to share,
And on which to shine a light.

Dyslexia Is A Blessing Not A Curse

Dyslexia has been a blessing not a curse.
It has made me infinitely better not worse.
I see the world beyond the words.
And feel the life beyond the verse.
My language skills are not reversed.
And although my spellings look diverse.
My knowledge of the language is not inverse.

The MelonCollie

A rare and unseen beast,
Just like the Lock Ness monster.
Mythical in existence,
Unheard of by its nature.
With the anatomy of a dog,
And the flesh of a water melon.
Something clearly wrong,
With this animal creation.
The product of a dyslexic slip,
Followed by a quick wit.
Ended up creating something,
That should really not exist.

Pets

The Potato Hider

Let me tell you the tale,
Of a Labrador,
Whose dream was hiding tubers.
She'd steal from the bag,
And hide what she had,
Around the house for later.
Jacky was her name,
With a cunning little brain,
Her hoard was potatoes.
Even after she passed,
Potatoes grew on the grass,
Where they had never been planted.

Black Spot

Some say a black cat,
Is a sign of bad luck.
Like the black spot,
On a pirates hand.
Spot was no black mark,
She didn't have a bad heart.
Spot was one of a kind,
A real furry princess.
Self-sufficient hunter,
Fiercely loyal purrer.
A cat like no other,
The purrfect little stunner.

A Smudge on Our Hearts

There is a small cat paw,
Smudged on our hearts.
An indelible mark,
Created by years of care,
For a cat no longer here.
***
Our little Smudge,
His nine lives spent,
Has gone to sleep,
For his final rest,
Having breathed his last breath.

Our Little Star

Twinkle twinkle,
Little Star,
What a wonderful,
Dog you were.
A little black lab,
So bright,
Like a shining,
happy light,
Twinkle twinkle,
Little star,
How I miss,
Who you were.

Living to the Max

My not so little lab,
Showed me what life was about,
He would run wild,
Eat what he could,
Sleep when he should,
And do it all again tomorrow.
***
He would run at me,
Mouth open wide,
Tongue hanging out,
Not trying to hide,
His excitement,
Of seeing me outside.
***
There is nothing like a dog,
To show you of life,
How to have no cares,
Love everyone here and there,
And most importantly,
How to live to the Max.

Soft Sophie

Little Sophie,
With her floppy ears,
Soft fur,
And little cares,
Tail wagging,
Here and there,
Grinning from,
Ear to ear.

The Sock Stealer

We once had a pup who liked socks,
And he would steal whatever he caught.
He'd grab from the washing,
And then you'd hear running.
He'd make for the bed,
Then duck his head,
And hide under the frame.

***

This started as a puppy,
And he grew fairly lanky.
Came the time,
For his last dash and dine.
He grabbed a sock,
And made for the spot,
But his head hit the frame,
And he never did it again.

Our Little Poppy

Our little Poppy,
So delicate and small,
A collie without sense,
Or intelligence at all.
***
You never tire of playing,
And beg us never-ending,
To go to the park,
With your favourite ball.
***
You are at our feet,
In the evening,
And come to us,
Before we call.
***
You're our little puppy,
With your little paws,
And you know how,
To make us aww.

Storm in a Teacup

Some pets have brains,
And some have brawn,
You had neither,
And that just seemed wrong.
***
But what you lacked in both,
you made up for with energy,
You could run rings around,
All the other puppies.
***
Life with you,
Was a never ending story,
One that I'm sure the cats,
Were glad was only temporary.

Garfield

Gorgeous cat,
Always able to bring a smile.
Right form when we,
First laid eyes on him,
I knew he would be a good cat.
Each memory is amazing,
Like a never-ending dream,
Didn't want to wake up from.

Love so Skye High

There is no love I know,
Like the love a dog shows,
Unending, unchanging and always known.
*
Nowhere is the limit,
For the love a dog shows,
Not here not there not the Skye.
*
So I take this time to note,
The love we both shared,
The many years of fetch,
The many years of care.
*
But dear Skye,
Don't take this as goodbye,
But more as a,
Till we meet again.

Animals

Cat Among The Pigeons

Meow Meow Meow,
Meow Meow,
Meow Meow,
Meow Meow Meow,
Meow Meow.

                              Tweet Tweet Tweet,
                                      Tweet Tweet.
                      Tweet Tweet Tweet Tweet,
                                      Tweet Tweet.

              Meow,
           Tweet Tweet,
           Meow Meow,
      Tweet Tweet Tweet,
          Meow Tweet,
          Tweet Meow,
             Meow!
TWEET Tweet Tweet Tweet tweet tweet twe-ugh,
             Purr.

Ladybug

Sat on a rock,
At the height of the day,
Is a little spotty friend,
Whiling the time away,
Just waiting for aphids,
To chew upon,
It rests and waits,
For dinner to come,
It's alliteral little laidback ladybug.

Lion

The king of the animal kingdom,
The empress of the savanna empire,
In a monarchy that includes jaguars.
***
The lion is a proud prowler,
While being a stealthy stalker,
Doing everything with natural ease.

Seagull

The brunch bandit,
Just waiting for your back to turn,
To ruin your life,
In a food hit and run.

***

They know just what they want,
And even if it's your croissant,
They'll stop at nothing,
To get their prize.

***

So keep an eye,
Up on the skies,
And protect your food,
From that noisy brood.

Humans

God's greatest experiment,
Or evolutions current form?
Either way we can agree,
We are all humans as one.
***
All have different stories,
Come from different places,
Going to our own destinations,
Filling our own spaces.
***
We are all perfect,
In our own ways,
Each and every one of us,
No matter what others say.

Platypus

Platypus,
The jokes on us,
Bill of a bird,
With not feathers,
But fur.
***
Once berated,
As but a hoax,
There are few of us,
That do not know the,
Platypus.

Cat

Proud prowler in the garden,
Lazy lion in the house,
When required demands attention.
Always willing to catch the mouse.
***
Pet to many,
Allergy to few,
Not always friendly,
Can make someone bless you.
***
Furless at times,
Fearless at others,
Will play with your mind,
And sleep on your covers.

Mouse

Me eat your jam,
Me eat your cheese,
Me eats whatever I please.
***
Me squeak all day,
Me squeak all night,
Me squeak whenever I like.
***
Me goes here,
Me goes there,
Me goes wherever I care.

Dog

An ancient pet,
A friend of man,
Often a helping hand.
***

A fierce companion,
A loyal friend,
Often with love to lend.
***

A member of family,
A part of the plan,
There to bring a smile whenever it can.

Magpie

A bearer of bad tidings,
A curse on the wing,
The black and white mischief,
Collecting shiny things.

***

A rattle for a voice,
That never whispers,
A call to send shivers,
Down the spines of listeners.

***

We all know the rhyme of old,
For the number of silver and of gold,
How many for a girl and a boy,
And of the secret ought not to be told.

Caterpillar

Proof that great change,
Is not done easily,
But can have,
Beautiful,
Side effects,
For you and me,
And the world to see.

Dragonfly

The helicopter of the insect world,
Once grew to the size of the absurd.
A majestic flyer in the sky,
A deadly stalker flying by,
There is nothing quite like a dragonfly.

Flowers

Daffodil

A sure fire sign,
That spring has sprung,
The grass banks of gold,
The front yards of yellow.

***

These hardy wee bulbs,
Clustered together,
Once blanketed with snow,
Now open their show.

***

A short-lived display,
Of summer on its way,
With the passing of winter,
And the days that were bitter.

Rose

A rose is not defined,
By the thorns that line it's sides.
It is not renowned,
With the rough barklike surround.
We don't vilify the flower,
For the stalk that holds it skyward.
It's the beauty we remember,
And the delicate velvety texture.
***
A rose conjures connotations,
Of bright garish colours,
And fragrant variations.
Of gardens of red,
And flowers of love,
Of a parting gift,
To those above.
***
Each rose a symbol,
Of a different thing,
Stirring thoughts,
Of wedding rings,
And marriage,
And final goodbyes.
Each rose has meaning,
In somebodies eyes.

Dandy Lion

As bright as a summers sun,
Sitting in my lawn,
Out of place,
Taking up space,
An annoying little thorn.

***

A stunning yellow flower,
When sitting in a pot,
A pain in the path,
When growing in the grass,
And very hard to stop.

Lily

Unlike a lily,
The colours of the rainbow,
Cannot be contained.
*

Although smell as rich,
The lilies in a bouquet,
Seldom are as sweet.
*

Such soft petals,
Amongst the green in a vase,
Of soft white lilies.
*

Happiness is found,
In a well-choreographed vase,
Of beautiful lilies.

Daisy

The first jewellery worn by children,
Made in chains by friends,
Picked from gardens in the sun,
In summers that seemed to never end.
***
A simple white crown of petals,
Surrounding the yellow stone,
Daisy chains could be so weak,
Back then they seemed so strong.
***
The jewel that made my childhood,
Now just a summer weed,
Growing amongst the garden lawn,
Just waiting to be mown.
***
Those days seem far away now,
Just like a distant memory,
But when I think about them,
My heart returns home.

Tulip

To you,
Undervalued little flower,
Like a teardrop growing upwards,
Interesting in all your forms,
Plantae grown from a bulb.

Thistle

Oh flower of Scotland,
A sign of my home,
I could be a world away,
And I'd still hear your song.
***
Grown on the mountain sides,
From where I belong,
Strong and sturdy,
To rough out the storms.
***
But somehow still tender,
With your purplish hue,
A reminder of where,
My heart belong to.

Rhododendron

The old lady of the garden,
keepers her patch clear,
With beautiful bouquets,
She wears in her hair,
A stunning green bush,
That once a year,
Brightens up the flower bed,
And brings garden cheer.

Fruit Rhyme

What is a Fruit

What is a fruit,
I put to you,
Is it sweet,
And full of juice,
Or is it just,
A seeded sprout,
That's used to spread,
seeds about.
Whatever you say,
I have no doubt,
A fruits a fruit,
I will shout,
So let's move on,
And start this show,
Welcome to,
The fruit only poets grow.

Strawberry

What a Great, British fruit,
The Strawberry is,
All red and plump,
With a soft juicy skin,
Get a bit of cream,
And you will be ready for Wimbledon.

Pomegranate

I sit and eat pomegranate,
In the city of granite,
On the third planet,
From the sun,
***
I like Pomegranate,
It is taken for granted,
And should not be replaced,
with a carrot.

Banana

Ba-na-na-na-na-na-na-na
Fruit man,
Ba-na-na-na-na-na-na-na
Fruit man, Fruit man,
***
All yellow and long,
With a curve,
That's not wrong,
And a white flesh inside,
Tasty and sweet,
A fruit to eat,
Nom nom nom.

Banana (ALT)

Oh what such a fruit,
Grows on a herb,
Enjoyed with cereal,
It's that absurd,
Sometimes Straight,
But quite often curved,
Let's give a cheer,
For this amazing fruit,
That grows on a herb.

Kiwi

So round and green,
Fuzzy and gooey,
Kiwi is all nice and juicy.
***
With a spoon,
Or all at once,
Have one with your lunch.
***
In a smoothie,
Or in one bite,
I think I'll have one tonight.

Tomato

You say it's not so,
But I know tomato,
Is a fruit not a veg,
So let it be said,
Now give it a rest,
It's a fruit nothing less.

Cherry

Cherry rhymes with Sherry,
And also with berry,
But not with carpet.
Cherry is very,
Sweet like a berry,
But not hairy like carpet.

Lime

I see the Lime light,
That's not a crime like,
I like the late night,
With a Lime bite.
***
Bitter and sweet,
All citrusy and sharp,
Just like a bad night,
Out in the Lime light.

Durian

There he ran,
The durian,
All spiky and squishy.
***
It stinks,
It stings,
Growing up there in the tree.
***
All green,
And spiny,
Don't fall on me.

Lemon

Lemon like lime,
Tastes just fine.
Lemons are sweet,
And taste really neat.
Lemons can juice,
Or spread loose.

Pineapple

Probably underrated,
Inevitably misunderstood,
Never written about,
Except to grumble,
About its appearance on,
Pizzas with ham,
Pineapple should be,
Loved by,
Everyone.

Pineapple (ALT)

Pineapples are golden,
But they are not a fruit,
From the Bromeliaceae Family,
They are in-fact many fruit.
*

Your many berries,
Have many uses,
From hats to salads,
And even to juices.
*

I love a pineapple,
With my boyfriend,
Especially before,
A fun weekend...

Lemons and Life

You are told in life,
"If life gives you lemons,
Make lemonade."
But what about,
"Don't take things from strangers,"
From this I say,
Life is a friend,
Greet it each day,
With a smile,
A hand,
And love it day-by-day.

Temporary Things

Sea Wave

A wise man once said,
Life is like a wave,
A temporary rearrangement of molecules,
Into a structure with meaning.
***

When the wave crashes,
Those molecules return,
To the sea,
To be used again.
***

Never in the same arraignment,
Always unique in their configuration,
Creating a new wave every time,
With its very own design.
***

A wave is temporary,
And cannot be recreated,
Each moment of it should be enjoyed,
Each second should be celebrated.

Bubble

You know that fleeting moment,
In which you see a bubble,
There one minute,
Popped the next,
With little in the way of left.
***
It mimics a wave,
Crashing on a beach,
Where we know,
For certain,
The wave won't reform.
***
Few things feel as final,
As a bubble popping,
A wave crashing,
Loved one passing,
Not to be remade again.
***
Watch that bubble closely,
Don't let it leave your eye,
When it's gone, it's gone,
And all you can say is,
Goodbye.

Life

There are few things in time,
As temporary as life.
A snapshot in time,
Where for a brief moment,
The universe can think for itself.
***
The arraignment of stardust,
Into each and every one of us.
It's both a blessing and a curse,
That life is so short,
And yet so diverse.
***
No one of us is safe,
From the sands of fate.
In time we each become,
No matter where we're born,
Dust beneath the sun.
***
Learn to enjoy life,
For it is a double edged knife.
Here one day,
And gone the next,
Finished in a single breath.

Winer Frost

In the late depth of,
The darkest of,
The cold of,
Winter.

*

The,
Hard frost,
Glints in silver,
And crunch in step.

*

The words of winter,
Spoken by the soil,
Hardened by,
Frost.

*

Crunch,
In the step,
Of each foot,
On winter's ground.

Summer Breeze

That whisper upon your cheek,
Like the warm kiss,
When you lift a cup of tea.
***
It reminds you of the softness,
That summer can bring,
The opposite of the nip,
Of the winter wind.
***
The gentle caress,
Of summers hands,
Against your face.
***
The season's way of saying,
It will be there for you,
After the long dark months,
Of earth's orbit-imposed curfew.
***
But don't stay too long,
In the sun's love,
It may give you more,
Of a burning hug.

Seasons

Yellow rainbow upon the soil,
On that bright spring day.
Purple hue upon the hills,
On that worm summers day.
Brown squishy mess upon the roads,
On that dull autumn day.
Whirlwind whitewash upon the ground,
On that cold Christmas day.
***
Autumn leaves on Summer trees,
Honey bees on Autumn leaves,
Time moves on so we might see,
Those honey bees on Autumn leaves,
And Autumn leaves on Summer trees,
When we wake tomorrow.

Fireworks

Some make a bang,
Some go with a pop,
And some make more light,
Than sound when they go off.
***
Whether their rockets,
Candles or Catherine wheels,
Or some mix of the three,
The sound is sure to make you scream.
***
They mark New Year,
The whole world round,
And the 4th of July in the US,
And in the UK Guy Fawkes' death.
***
A bright bang,
And a loud flash,
Can be enough,
To bring a rush.

Time

I am the youngest I will ever be,
Yet the oldest I have ever seemed,
Stop the clock now,
And let time stand still.
***
For he is the reason,
Life is never dull,
But sometimes I need,
The clock to stop,
And time to leave me be.
***
But he marches on,
Tick by tock,
And tock by tick,
Endlessly to the metronome.
***
So cherish the time,
Because tomorrow as with now,
You will be the youngest you ever were,
But the oldest you have ever been.

Underneath These Stars

Underneath these stars,
We said our hellos.
The stars smiling down,
On only the heavens can know.
Who could have seen,
What was going to happen?
Who could have known,
I'd fall in love.
**

So underneath these stars I greet you,
Underneath these stars I'll meet you,
Underneath these stars I'll kiss you,
So only us and them will know.
**

Underneath these stars,
We are equal.
The stars see us,
As just people,
What would they say,
About what we have?
Is it ok,
For two men to fall in love?
**

Underneath these stars I miss you,
Underneath these stars I love you,
Underneath these stars I'll kiss you.
When you come back home to me.
**

Underneath these stars,
People will try and tare us apart.
When they do,
Just look at the stars.
And they will lead you home to me.
Our love is as real,
As you let your heart feel,
Only let the stars judge,

And the world can never hurt you.
**

Underneath the stars we're equal,
Underneath the stars their equal,
Underneath the stars they can't judge you,
Unless you let them.
**

So underneath these stars I'll love you,
And underneath these stars I'll hug you,
While underneath these stars I'll kiss you,
And let you hold my hand in yours.

The Simple Things

All I want,
Are the simple things,
Your hands on my back,
Your arms round my waist.
*

All I seek,
Is you next to me,
Your heartbeat matching mine,
It being the only thing keeping time.
*

All I need,
Is our eyes to meet,
And I will feel complete,
Knowing nothing will hurt me.
*

All I wish,
Is for you this Christmas,
Under the white mistletoe,
In my arms with our love in your eyes.
*

All at once,
My dream will be complete,
My heart for you and your heart for me,
One life together and that life our own,
No pain or fear,
Just us growing old together.
*

All I want,
Are the simple things,
Like you lying next to me.

Ode to the Elements

Earth ▽

Some cultures know it,
As earthly mother,
Others as father.
It is the solid,
Beneath our feet.
The things that,
Grounds us all.
The root of all life,
And the inevitable end.

Air △

Once associated with Blood,
And the season of spring,
The age of infancy,
And the liver beneath our skin,
With a temperament of sanguine.
***
Air is an ancient element,
With qualities and temperament,
Once conceived as warm and moist,
From the time of Plato and Aristotle,
A basic element of living life.

Fire △

Fire congers up images of passion,
An element of the Golden Dawn system.
It had practical uses in alchemy,
It is a mainstay of destruction.
Known for its transforming powers,
Taking wood from solid to ash.
Never underestimate the ability,
Of fire to burn.

Water ▽

One of the traditional four,
It marked the boundary on the floor,
Between the air within the sky,
And the earth beneath where you lie.
***
Associated with emotion,
And also intuition,
Plato saw it as tiny balls,
Ungraspable in our paws.
***
A fundamental part of life,
Without which there would be strife,
A binding need of all humanity,
Without which we'd lose our sanity.

Metal

Although not,
A medieval tradition element,
It still features,
As an element in tradition.
***
Often linked with autumn,
And the play thing of alchemists,
With the never ending dream,
Of turning led to gold.
***
Metal has held the hearts,
In the form of a ring,
Or saved hearts,
In the form of a syringe.
***
A mainstay of modern science,
Still the point of elemental research,
With many more secrets,
Still out of our reach.

Wood

Let me whittle you a story,
Of a material so strong,
That empires were once built on.
***
Naturally grown in forests,
Strong enough to hold back water,
But playable in the right hands.
***
Nature's hair upon the earth,
Plucked by man,
To be put to work.
***
In innumerable shapes and sizes,
From mountain to the sea,
There are many uses for a tree.

Love Poems

Another Time or Another Place

In another time,
Or another place,
We could have been great.
But we live in this time,
And this place,
And so I must face,
A world without you.

***

My heart longs for you,
As so many hearts do,
Wishing to take you on a date.
But my heart is blue,
It feels broken in two,
And it know the cue,
It must bid you ado.

You're one of a Kind

Your one of a kind,
Not one in a million,
Not even one in a billion.
***
When you were made,
The gods looked down,
With a smile on their face.
***
You are the only one,
To make my heart skip,
And cause a smile form cheek to cheek.
***
Without a word,
From your mouth,
You make the world right.
***
There is nothing like your grace,
To put everything in place,
On a cold dark night.

Why I Love the UK

I've felt the summer sun glow,
and the cold nip of snow,
I've heard the autumn deer call,
and watched the fawns crawl,
I've seen the rain fall,
***
and the rainbow tall,
I've smelt the honeydew there,
and smelt the cold winter air,
I've tasted the meat of the highlands,
and the fruits of the lowlands,
These things I say,
Remind me why,
I love the UK.

Acrostic Love Poem

Right when I had given up,
Over you came,
Bringing me to love again,
***
Because of you,
Everything feels new,
Every day feels good,
Come hug me now,
Reach for my heart,
Only let me go when you have to,
For now I'm thinking of you,
Think of me to.

I Dream

I dream as does any man,
I dream of life,
Of money,
But mostly of you.
***
Our lives together,
Lived as one,
Our dreams shared,
Every one,
***
A life together,
Of love and laughter,
Happiness and Hugs,
From now ever after.

I Am a Lucky Man

Very few people are as lucky as me,
I have my love at my side,
My family in my life,
And friends around,
***
I would be nothing without my man,
Although I don't say it much,
I love him beyond all measure,
And I know he loves me back,
***
Family is a strong thing,
And mine is no exception,
We stand with each other,
Through thick and thin,
***
And who would I be,
Without the friends who complete me,
Although there are few,
They are close and dear.
***
When I'm feeling down,
Or stressed at life,
I just remember,
There are those not as lucky as me.

Hope

Hope,
Is not just a useless word,
It has endless meaning,
Freedom,
Is not an actless sentiment,
It keeps us breathing.
***
We all live in hope,
To live in freedom,
When freedom is taken for granted,
Hope is ignored,
And one by one,
People become,
Mindless hordes,
Living for tomorrow,
Saving for today,
Having nothing to their name.
***
Hope
Is not just a useless word,
It gives the world meaning,
Love,
Is a binding force,
That keeps hearts beating.
***
We all live in hope,
To find true love,
Which shows our blindness,
Love not just your partner,
With true love,
Love your neighbour,
Your father,
Your fellow humans,
With the same love,
And the world will be,
As it should.

What I Would Give

You could recite python,
Without missing a beat,
Make me smile,
From cheek to cheek,
Put me in stitches,
For over a week,
And say you love me,
As big as the street,
Now what I would give,
To hear goodnight one last time.

You could make eggs,
With a runny yoke,
Find the right time,
To tell the perfect joke,
Tried to fix things,
Or just give them a poke,
And say I love you,
As big as you know,
Now what I would give,
To say goodnight one last time.

This Old Heart of Mine

Given the world,
I would give it away,
Just to spend my time,
Lying next to you each day.
*

I have had many days to myself,
And not one of them compares,
To a single hour with you.
**

But you don't see me,
And although I may be a young guy,
My heart is old and waiting for you,
I just want to love you in the old fashioned way,
Long nights lying together,
Just in each other's company.
**

Life in my mind,
Seemed easier before,
But now I spend every day,
Just longing for you to be with me.
*

What I would give for just a kiss,
To feel your lips on mine,
And the warmth of your breath,
**

But you don't see me,
And I am starting to think,
You never will,
My heart will forever long for yours
But it knows the drill,
Smile and move on like before.
*

But you don't see me,
And although I may be a young guy,
My heart is old and waiting for you,
I just want to love you in the old fashioned way,

Long nights lying together,
Just in each other's company.
*

Maybe one day you will see me,
But until then I must wait,
And live tomorrow as another day.

Open That Tin Heart

Over the years,
I thought I'd found love,
But it hadn't been true.
Then along came,
Someone completely different,
And that was you.
Never did I consider,
You could be for me,
And save me from becoming bitter.
Now five years on,
I don't look back,
On time that's gone.
My heart became tin,
With the hurt of time,
And you opened it for me.

Light of My Life

Years passed where I asked for you,
And who knew,
You were asking for me too.
***
We may not have known each other,
But our hearts knew,
you were asking for me,
And I was asking for you too.
***
My mornings are bright,
Waking next to you,
Seeing your smile,
Just being with you,
***
Once my nights were dark,
But you see,
You are a light,
In my life to me.

Today I Thought Of You

I thought of you today,
That is nothing new,
But I cannot tell you.
***
You were always there,
And I never knew,
How much I'd miss you.
***
So in the words you loved,
Life's a piece of shit,
When you look at it.
***
Without you here,
I'll live by your ways,
And enjoy my life.

If Life Were

If life were a song,
I'd sing it for you,
Every line that I'd sing,
Would bleed and run true.
*
If life were a play,
I'd act it with you,
Every line that I'd say,
Would be just for you.
*
If life were a talk,
I'd speak it for you,
Every word that I'd say,
Would be to love you.
*
Alas life is just life,
This much is true,
So please let me spend,
Every moment with you.

Te Amo

Te amo my morning sun,
I love you my evening light,
The first thing I think about in the morning,
The final thing I think about at night.

Winter of Love

As the nights grow cold,
The leaves on the trees grow weary,
But the heart grows warm,
And the legs grow steadfast.
*

Where the certainty of the winter,
The lining of frost,
And the snow falls,
Now grow the uncertainty of love.
*

The heart calls,
The leaves fall,
The mind feels,
The wind knows,
All will be well in the end.

Love Is Like a Song

Like music from an orchestra,
Like strings that are plucked,
Love vibrates around us,
Love is in all of us.
***
In a whisper,
Or in a shout,
Love lives within us,
We just need to let it out.
***
Feel it in you,
Feel it fill you up,
Don't hide from love,
And don't hold it back.

We Once Said I Love You

You once said I love you without force,
Without pain, without remorse,
What we had was special,
But the bitterness came,
First it was just arguing,
Behind locked doors, then in public.
***
I once said I love you without wincing,
Without a sigh, without rolling my eyes,
What we had felt right,
But the cruelty came,
And we drifted apart,
Lived separately, then moved apart.
***
We once said I love you without spite,
Without sarcasm, without venom,
What we had worked,
But what finally came,
And finally ended it,
Was sharp words, and harsher jibes.

Will Boys Just Be Boys

Will boys just be boys,
Or girls just be girls,
Or can't people be people,
In our small little world.
***
Why do genders have to be genders,
And not girls be like boys,
Or boys be like girls,
Or just let people be people.
***
Can't we look beyond gender,
And see the person,
Who likes pink and Buffy,
But is still a straight man.
***
Care not for the sex,
And ignore the gender,
Stand shoulder to shoulder,
And never surrender.
***
We are all human,
The same under the skin,
Red blood flowing through,
The veins within.
***
We are born the same,
Have the same needs,
Expel the same waste,
And leave the same way.
***
Love people as people,
That's all we need,
Don't act out of hate,
Respect, love and be great.

For You

I only wish that you could see,
What you really mean to me.
My heart beats harder,
With every thought of you.

*

I wish I could catch you,
Like a butterfly in a net.
But that is not to be,
I must use the tools given to me.

*

My poetry, every word for you.
My life, every breath for you.
My mind, every thought of you.
My day, every moment lived for you.

*

Let our love be a lifetime,
To know each other for ever,
To have our thoughts for each other,
And to live every moment to come together.

All I Want

I want to hug you
I just want to love you,
But I don't know how to tell you,
And would you even let me.
*

I want to lie next to you,
To just sleep beside you,
But I don't know how to ask,
And would you even want to.
*

I want to give you my hand,
Just give you my heart,
But I don't know how to approach you,
Where should I start.

Love Is

Love is not simple,
And love is not hard.
Love is not logical,
But love is not chaos.
Love is not complete,
But love is my incomplete.
Love is not fixed,
And love is my broken.
Love is the hand that helps you up,
And the hand that throws you down.
Love is a cry of happiness,
And a cry of pain.
Love is all these things at once,
But no matter what you feel amazing.

Love Is Like

Love is like,
A lifetime of learning.
Love is like,
A night full of tossing and turning.
Love is like,
Never knowing but never caring.
Love is like,
A spear to the chest.
Love is like,
Not being able to rest.
But most of all,
Love is Love whatever that is.

Sometimes All You Need Is Hello

People talk of the words,
"I love you"
As being all they need to feel whole,
But sometimes they forget,
The power of the simple word,
"Hello"

I Learned To Love From You

My heart was hardened before I met you,
And you softened it up,
Made me see I deserved love,
Made me feel I could love.

*

But now you have gone and fallen silent,
And my heart is growing still,
What have I done to push you away?
Will I ever know?

*

You have stolen my heart,
And left me alone,
Will I ever know,
How I pushed you away?

*

Just come to me and talk to me,
And maybe we can see this through,
But if we can't please don't worry,
I learned to love from you!

Love for the Now

We wait for love,
Until we can wait no more,
We don't look at what we've got,
Instead we look for what could be in store.
***
Life is simpler,
If you love what you have,
And don't think about what you want,
But be content in the now and thankful for the morrow.
***
Grab your friends,
Remind them you are there,
You will love them no matter what,
Let them know you have and always will care.

Guide Me Through

Take me from dark,
Right into the light,
Right through the day,
And into the night.
*

If love is the dark,
Then you are the light,
Taking me through the day,
And through the night.
*

Let me be in your arms,
That you may guide my way,
All through Valentine's night,
And Valentine's Day.

You Make the World Simple

The world is full of pain,
Fear, hate and war,
But with you here,
You make me forget it all.
***
Few things are impossible,
When we are together,
The world is forgotten,
And life is much better.
***
Every time I see you,
My heart turns to jelly,
And my every whim is,
Waiting for your command.
***
When the world gets busy,
And life gets confusing,
You sit with me and smile,
And everything is simple again.

Acrostic Valentine Request

With it coming up to Valentine's Day,
I had someone in mind,
Little did you know but,
Like so many others,
I am too scared to tell you,
And maybe you will see this,
Maybe you would say yes...
***
Just someone I loved,
Once before,
He is amazing but I was,
Not what he was for,
***
Maybe this year you will say yes,
And maybe this year I will find love,
Come what may I will not stop,
Looking for the one to love,
Every day forever more.
Once again I find myself,
Doing something foolish.
***
For you I wrote this,
Rather difficult,
Acrostic poem,
So you would know who sent it,
Even without me saying my name so now I'm just,
Really hoping you'll want to be my Valentine.

Better To Have Loved and Lost

Just for a moment,
Of your time,
Sit with me,
Even just for one rhyme,
Perhaps we can,
Have a meal or see a movie.
***
Whilst I know,
I may never be yours,
Let's just,
Learn about each other.
I understand we,
Are just friends and,
May that last forever.
***
He'll never know,
Exactly how I feel,
So I will just,
Keep dreaming,
Even if it is for nothing.
Tis better to have loved and lost,
Than never to have loved at all.

You Are Wonderful

Hey you there,
Yes you,
With eyes on this page.
You are special,
Don't forget,
That you are loved today.
You are wonderful,
You are,
And don't listen to naysayers.
You are amazing,
It's true,
My work lives through you.
There is only,
One you,
Live as the true you.
I am blessed,
With love,
That you read my work.

Give Me a Movie

Give me a movie,
Make it my life,
Why do they have,
All the happy ending,
And all the happily ever afters.
*
Make my life like a movie,
Why can't it just be,
Drama, life and love,
Ending just as it should,
Just like a wish.
*
Life is not a movie,
And why should it be,
Love, work and life.
Ending as it will be,
Just as it should be.

Crime of Love

No one can see the future,
No one can see the time,
No one can see the crime.
*

To steal someone's heart,
Lock it up tight,
Is considered beautiful,
Until something doesn't go right.
*

Even through the time,
Even through the crime,
Even through the pain.
*

I'd still do it all again,
Give my heart up,
To be locked away,
Who wouldn't want to be loved that way.

Mines Is a Redhead

Some like the blonds,
Some like the brunets,
But I'm not like them,
I like the reds.
*

Some call them weird,
Some suggest sun cream,
Some call them beetroot,
But to they are my dream.
*

One day I will meet him,
And one day we will be,
In love and together,
Forever and ever.

My Love for You

My love for you has only grown,
Over the years and over the miles,
I have never stopped loving you.
My heart has been yours,
Since we first said hello,
Since you first let me know.
And after all this time,
You will understand,
The way my heart demands.
Some would have given up,
And some think I'm silly,
But I still love you.
My heart calls for you,
And sings continually,
I Love You...

Keep an Open Heart

If you close your heart,
And close your head,
You won't feel hurt,
You won't feel dread,
For love will never get to you,
And you will never fell new.

*

Love is worth a thousand tears,
Don't fear to lose them,
Don't fear to dread,
Just love the now,
And love the moment,
Love your heart,
And love your head,

*

Never live in fear,
Or live in dread,
Let your heart feel,
If you have that someone now,
You know the love I speak of,
But if you don't,
Then don't fret,
Just let your heart lead you to love.

*

Tonight before you go to bed,
Remember this,
You need your heart,
You need your head,
To feel that love,
Just ignore the dread.

Love (Read between the Lines)

Grab your heart and don't bottle it up.
Love isn't only for the strong.
By loving you will learn.
The many ways a heart breaks.
Horns and devil tales may plague you.
And people may even leave you.
Hold your own and keep on searching.
On the wishes of you heart and on your longings.
Tight in the knowledge you will find love.

Letting Go Of Love

You stole my heart,
From within my chest,
Ripped it out,
From beneath my breast.
***
Never knowing,
What you had done,
Had doomed my heart,
From then on.
***
I struggle to stop,
And let you go,
Because you are the only thing,
I now know.
***
But like a fallowed field,
Or a cold winter meadow,
My heart has started to clog up,
And I must let you go.
***
Don't forget me,
When you think,
Look back fondly,
From time to time.
***
I'll miss you,
My loving friend,
Even if you,
Were never truly mine.

Affirmation of Love

I love where no one loves,
I have love for the unloved,
Harm can't get to me as long as I feel love,
Only what is for my divine good can touch me,
And in all situations remind me to love,
As with love pain can be healed.

You Were My Dream

There were nights I would sleep,
And wish I wouldn't wake,
Seeing you with me,
Meant waking was heartache.
***
Some people said I was silly,
But all I wanted was you with me,
I knew it wasn't meant to be,
Just you with me, you see.
***
You made me fearless,
Happy to let go from it all,
You will never know,
How I feel when you call.
***
Life will never be the same,
Knowing you won't love me,
The way I love you,
There will never be a me and you.

Weak at the Knees

Weak at the knees,
Sweet begins to bead,
I know you are there,
But you will never be here.
***
You had the eyes the smile,
The love and the style,
My taste in music,
It was all there.
***
But my mind was aching,
You weren't mine,
For the taking,
Just a friend for the making.
***
You will always make,
Me weak at the knees,
Make me fall in a breeze,
But you will never be with me.

He FriendZoned Me

I fell for him,
Like the leaves,
Did for the autumn,
I made a move,
With great intention,
I wanted to love him,
I wanted to be his,
He smiled and said,
Were just good friends,
I don't want to ruin this,
We agreed and I left,
I wish we were together,
But it could never be,
As he FriendZoned me.

The Last Words (Before the First Kiss)

Waiting is not fun,
Given its for you,
You don't know it yet,
But I'm after you.
*

Too many years of fighting
Fighting in my head,
Too many tears and too much dread.
*

I have done all,
I have seen you fall,
I have felt your highs,
And seen your lows.
*

Too many years of fighting,
Fighting in my head,
Too many tears to let this go on.
*

Even after this time,
I hear them ring in my head,
Will it be the last words,
Before the dread or,
The last words before the first kiss.
***

Too many years of fighting,
All the fighting in my head,
Too many years of the same words,
Ringing in my head,
Too many tears, time to let it go,
I love you now I know I won't live in dread.

Oddity of Love

Is it not strange,
How we focus on an organ,
At the centre of the body.

*

The pump of life,
As the control of love,
At the centre of our life.

*

It's strange we say,
Each beat for each other,
And our heart in another's hands.

Love in Actions

Given a word,
I'll make it a song.
Given a world,
I'll make it a stage.
Given a day,
I'll make it a memory.
Given a life,
I'll make it amazing.
Given a heart,
I'll cherish it forever.
Given a dream,
I'll make it a reality.
And given your hand,
I'll hold it forever and never let go.

I Will Always Love You

I was only kidding myself,
When is was thinking about you,
Because don't you see,
Why would someone like you,
Be thinking about someone like me.
*

Our hearts are in the right place,
But that's not together,
We could never be,
Not while you don't have feelings,
For this lonely wreck that is me.
*

I have prayed for you,
Wished you'd see,
How much you,
Really mean to me,
To me.
*

I love you dear friend,
But now I see,
I don't think I can live like this,
With feelings for you,
While you don't have feelings for me,
*

You have been a great friend,
But I know what I must do,
Thank you for all the good times,
Have a good life and please remember,
I will always love you.

Just Wish I Could Ask

Just thinking to myself,
On the past two years.
Should I ask you,
Even though I know,
Pretty much,
How the situation would go.
***
Wishing is just dreaming,
I know that already,
Love is not one sided,
Let it join you together,
In life there are two options,
Ask and be satisfied or,
Mope around and wait.
***
He probably won't see,
Even if he does,
Still should I ask him.
Kneeling I would say,
Eternally be mine,
That will never happen,
Though I just wish I could ask him.

Words of Love

If I could write a poem that would make you love me,
I would have written it already.
If I could write a song that would make you see,
How much you really mean to me.
If words could only make you feel,
The way I feel for you.
But songs and poems and words of love,
Never mean as much as a hug.

Letters

To A Loving Mum

Mothers are truly unique,
You get just one,
That one you keep.
***

Although things were sometimes tough,
And times looked more than rough,
You were always there to see us through.
***

Mums are not just mothers,
There sisters and carers,
Doctors and huggers.
***

So thank you mum,
For being just you,
And all the amazing things you do.

To My Special Man

Dear diary, one day, I dreamed,
A man, I'd meet, it seemed,
You did come along,
And played like a song,
Like you did in all my dreams.

To An Old Crush

I crushed on you so hard,
That the sight of your name on my phone,
Or the sound of your voice in my ear,
Would have been enough to make,
My heart beat all year.
***
And although my feelings were my own,
Not to be shared by you,
You could always make my heart beat true,
***
I write this letter today,
Having never gotten away,
From those feeling for you,
But having learned to accept,
You as a very close friend.

To My Late Dad

People ask me why I cry,
It's because I never got to say goodbye.
We spoke for hours on and off,
And would end it with a "right I'm off".
Sometimes we would "see you later",
And sometimes end it "alligator".
But it was impossible for me to see,
What goodbye was going to be.
And as such I never said the words,
Goodbye my father, love, your son.

Goodbye to another Family Member

Rest now your tired eyes,
You have lived and loved,
And now head for the skies.
***
We won't meet again,
Until I join you in heaven,
When I am called by him.
***
For now you must know,
A part of me has now gone,
And will follow you there.
***
We will miss you here,
Until we are together,
Goodbye to another family member.

To A Loving Family

Life is not all sunshine and roses,
There are things that go right,
And things that go wrongses.
But what makes life a little easier,
Is having a family who love,
And make things a little cheesier.
To you my family I say this,
Thanks for the love,
And thanks for the bliss.
Without you all there would be little,
Life would be cold,
And I would be brittle.
I love you all with all my heart,
You love effortlessly,
Like some kind of art.

To My Dog

No matter how dark,
No matter how bleak,
I come home to you,
And I hear you squeak.
***
You stomp and pad,
Which drives me mad,
But also makes,
My heart glad.
***
From the moment I held you,
Till the moment we sleep,
I love watching you,
Eat, drink and be sweet.
***
You know when I'm down,
Or I'm wearing a frown,
You will come up,
And make a cute sound.

To The One My Heart Wants

I sit here thinking,
What do you think?
My heart always seeking,
Your hand in mine.
*

Will this ever happen?
Could this ever be?
I can but wish and dream,
You will be lying next to me.
*

We only met two years ago,
And still I feel my heart enthralled,
What magic have you cast over me?
And how can I break this spell?
*

I have a thousand wards to tell you,
And not one of them has the courage,
To jump out and say what they must,
When I am in your presence.
*

Have you ever wondered?
What I have so often wondered,
How a night together would feel,
And what a night in each other's arms would do.
*

My dreams are filed with you,
My days are filled with hope of seeing you,
My work is to impress you,
And my every poem is to catch your eye.
*

You will never know this was written for you,
You may never know how much I love you,
I just wish I could let you know but I am scared,
Maybe this year you will tell me I pray.

To The One That Got Away

You left an indelible,
Line on my heart,
And although we didn't,
End up together,
You will always stay,
Etched on my heart.
***
You taught me to be,
The real version of me,
And not to worry about,
The way the world saw,
The man that I was,
And the man I wanted to be.
***
So take the thanks from me,
For being so you,
And for helping me understand,
That life is too short,
To worry about,
What the world will become.

The End

Last But Not Least

And finally,
Last but by no means least,
Here is my final piece,
My bowing down,
Before the curtain,
Because something now is certain.
***
The book is done,
The poems all gone,
All that's left,
Is my swan song,
And one last so long,
Before I face the final curtain.
***
It's goodbye for now,
Let me make one last vow,
My promise to you,
More poems somehow,
Should life allow,
But I'll do it my way.

About The Author

William Fraser or better known as the Pesky Poet started out on the journey of writing in 2012 as a way of proving that his recent dyslexia identification did not mean the death of a writing career.

At that point in 2012 William was writing about the London Olympics under the pen name Creatively Become Indifferent. Since then he has gone through a change of pen name and has touched on topics ranging from Unrequited Love and the Loss of Family.

In the last couple of years William's father was taken at the young age of 51. The late Mr Fraser was an avid supporter of William perusing his dreams and was one of the backing supporters of Creatively Become Indifferent and Pesky Poetry.

The loss of his father has turned William back to looking at past poems and pushed him to write new material. This ultimately has led to a melancholy in his heart which, through a tongue and cheek conversation, led to the MelonCollie in this book.

www.ingramcontent.com/pod-product-compliance
Lightning Source LLC
LaVergne TN
LVHW010301260326
834688LV00044B/1397